RIGHTEOUS INDIGNATION

Poems

Jabulani Mzinyathi

Edited by Tendai R. Mwanaka
Typeset by Tendai R Mwanaka
Cover: Mad Bob Republic/Cholera Republic © Tendai R Mwanaka

Mwanaka Media and Publishing Pvt Ltd,
Chitungwiza Zimbabwe

*

Creativity, Wisdom and Beauty

Publisher: Tendai R Mwanaka

Mwanaka Media and Publishing Pvt Ltd *(Mmap)*

24 Svosve Road, Zengeza 1

Chitungwiza Zimbabwe

mwanaka@yahoo.com

www.africanbookscollective.com/publishers/mwanaka-media-and-publishing

https://facebook.com/MwanakaMediaAndPublishing/

Distributed in and outside N. America by African Books Collective

orders@africanbookscollective.com

www.africanbookscollective.com

ISBN:978-1-77906-502-5

EAN:9781779065025

DISCLAIMER

All views expressed in this publication are those of the author and do not necessarily reflect the views of *Mmap*.

iii

CONTENTS TABLE

MIXED BAG

INTRODUCTION

These poems are rooted in the socio-politico and economic morass that has bedevilled my country of birth, Zimbabwe. The poems are in that sense organic. These poems are part of a continuum that commenced in the published collection entitled *Under The Steel Yoke*.

The poems are arranged under five parts namely *Against TheShitstem. In The Heroes Acre Of The Mind, Poems From The Setting Sun, The Spiritual Dimension* and *Mixed Bag*.

The *shitstem* is a term coined apparently by Peter Tosh [reggae singer, song writer]. Two words make it up, shit and system. The poet uses the term to express his displeasure at a corrupt system of governance that has been sustained through violence, hence images of dripping blood. The poet also expresses disgust at the mindless opulence that has the rich elite amassing wealth while the rest of the citizens wallow in abject poverty. This leads the poet in *Discourse* to say 'rivers of sewage flow ceaselessly.' It is against this background that the poet questions the use of the term 'honourable' when used in relation to those that have multiple farms while the landless villagers eke a living on dry barren land.

The poet questions the level of bootlicking or levels of sycophancy. There is the creation of the dangerous personality cult where mere mortals are deified. It is this realisation which leads the poet in *I Told You So* to say 'Assumed they owned that sacred struggle.' The poet also notes that there is what he calls television philanthropy. For political mileage some people are seen giving donations to the poor. The television cameras will be in tow. This is not how genuine giving should be portrayed. Those that give should not be like Pharisees that go to the top of mountains to be seen that they are praying.

The poet is keenly aware of the contributions of Zimbabwean poet Chenjerai Hove and states in *Poet In Exile* 'His voice deemed discordant' That poet relentlessly questioned the establishment. A question is asked of poet Denis Brutus regarding whether he left anything poetic about the xenophobia that bedevilled South Africa in his adopted home. Readers will do well to know he was born in the then Rhodesia[now Zimbabwe]. Surely he would have protested as much as he did against apartheid.

In the section entitled *Heroes Acre Of The Mind* the poet pays tribute to larger than life characters like Patrick Kombayi who played a prominent role in the liberation struggle. That he does not lie buried at Heroes Acre does not matter much for he lives on in some minds that know his role. The same equally applies to NdabaningiSithole. The poem *Yet Another Gap* is a tribute to Sithole. The story of liberation will have gaps if his role is not contextually mentioned. The poet thanks all heroes of the war of liberation in the poem *Thanking Liberators*. He quips though that their 'stories of triumph are spiced by the occasional innocuous lies.'

In this multi-faceted collection the poet questions the reviling of women over the natural menstrual cycle. He also questions the continued siphoning of resources to the erstwhile colonisers' capitals. Perhaps they are not erstwhile but still are alive and well and have just changed tactics to hoodwink the oppressed. The blame does not squarely lie on the ghosts of the past as stated in the poem *State Of The Continent*. In that poem the poet talks of graft/corruption. There is also righteous indignation aimed at megalomaniacs that have overstayed their welcome.

The poet still grapples with issues of spirituality and religion. He battles against apostasy. The poet has no kind words for those that are taking the unsuspecting and perhaps gullible for a ride through the warping of Christianity into what has become known as prosperity gospel. The poet expresses righteous indignation when he states in *Veiled Eyes* 'labelling our ways ancestral worship.' In another poem entitled *David Deadstone* the poet expresses indignation that David Livingstone had the audacity to call mosi-oa-tunya/shungunamutitima, Victoria Falls as if the BaTonga who first saw the world wonder did not matter.

In yet another poem playfully entitled *Mein Kampf*, the title of Adolf Hitler's book, the poet still battles for the reclamation of his spirituality. It is a rejection of the warped kind of Christianity that was used to bring subjugation to Africans. The kind of Christianity that termed African spirituality, pagan.

The poet has not embraced anger but righteous indignation. His poetry can be likened to a *jihad*. It is indeed a holy war against forces of evil that thrive where the masses wallow in abject poverty. The poet goes into international debate when he attacks the ICC which he derisively calls the international criminal conspiracy. The death of Saddam Hussein was never about weapons of mass destruction. It was Anglo–Saxon hegemony at work and also the plundering of oil in Iraq. Indeed these poems are a mixed bag.

AGAINST THE SHITSTEM

RIGHTEOUS INDIGNATION

This pen spits not venom
No venom against vermin
Driven it is by righteous indignation
Driven it is by an immense sense of justice
Echoing the words of Marcus Mosiah Garvey
That justice is greater than the law

The thoughts portrayed are organic
Travelling far and wide for wisdom
Learning lessons from Russia
Blame not the mirror if your face is askew
This mirror reflecting that wild dog snarl

A housefly cannot make honey
A bee cannot spread malaria
A dove can never crow
Blame me not for this righteous indignation
When the truncheon does its dance
Tearing up the flesh of perceived foes
When the smouldering tear gas canisters bounce
Scattering and choking those that dare shout
While an accusing finger points at the silent majority

I have not been able to bury my head in the sand
Refusing to carry that burden on my shoulders
I have not been able to admire the undulating landscape
Without thinking of many lying in unmarked graves

I have not been able to admire the setting sun
Without an invocation of images of dripping blood
This writing shall always be organic
After the funeral no longer shall there be dirges
A longing for the mirthful laughter of African children

GRAND MASTERS

Paulo Freire long said it
We have become adept
This has gone beyond aping
We have now raised the bar
As usually happens the students surpassed
Long surpassed their teacher

Where we used to call then baas
Where they were called masters
Chefs have now firmly entrenched themselves
Crude torture chambers now designed
Rights remain dead on the page
The pages of the many smoke screens

We are now the grand masters
Past masters at enslaving our own
Never letting crumbs fall off the tables
The high tables of our ostentation
On display the naked, shameless opulence
With inflated egos and arrogance in tow

CAUSTIC WORDS

There she was like a bull
A wounded buffalo bull on the rampage
Raw sewage flowed from her mouth
The stench of it filled my mind
Left me flummoxed beyond measure
The relentless unprovoked attack
The same tongue that praises the Lord
The same tongue that worships the devil
An attempt at mixing oil and water
Then she gored like a wounded buffalo
The nagging conscience she will bear
A giant emptiness engulfs her mind

DISCOURSE

When silence is mistaken for peace
In this unfolding tragicomedy
When the blind lead the one eyed
Then you ask why this soul is troubled

When rivers of sewage flow ceaselessly
When corruption becomes a national sport
And many are buried beneath mounds of poverty
Then you ask why my soul is troubled

When everywhere are the vibrations of violence
Brutality there on the pedestal placed
And the mark of the beast on their foreheads
And you ask why this soul is deeply troubled

TAKING IT FOR A JOKE

Perhaps there is therapy in it
When we take it for a joke
The putrid and ubiquitous foul stench
Firmly ensconced in society's nostrils
Perhaps it is about normalising the abnormal
For a state of equilibrium is the ultimate desire

We have termed it our national sport
As it devours our very souls
Like the leaping tongues of a veld fire
And now we take it for a joke
This cancer gnawing our very essence
There is an abundance of justification
And the state of equilibrium is reached

Everything now has a price tag
If they had their way they would
Packaging oxygen and selling to able buyers
And the poor would not live a day longer
Yes, they are already steeped in it
And we still take it for a big joke

HONOURABLE

Do I detect some irony here
When they call you honourable
When you are bereft of honour
When dishonour is your hall mark
That word mangled beyond recognition
The foul stench of dishonour everywhere
There in your fast imported cars
When the roads are pock marked
Like the victims of small pox
When you own multiple farms
While the landless are still the homeless
When they till the now tired, arid land
Where is your honour honourable sir, madam
When all you clamour for are diplomatic passports
To hide behind diplomatic immunity grabbing and stealing
To hide in diplomatic bags the stolen diamonds
While the people of Chiadzwa wallow in poverty
When billions of dollars vanish like dew in the morning
When this dissenting voice you brutally crush
With plastic bullets, water cannons, choking tear smoke
When the baton does its dance of death on my soul
And when all you do is wantonly destroy flora and fauna
Do I detect some irony here honourable sir, madam

THE SOUND OF EMPTINESS

What is the residue
Stripped of high sounding titles
Taken out of the limousines
Bereft of computerised wardrobes
Stripped of those suits from Harrods
And all the other fashion capitals of the world

What is the residue
Stripped of mindless ostentation
Perhaps a barren wind blowing
A drifting cloud bearing no rain
Maybe humility can fill the void

I TOLD YOU SO

Reality check time is now
That image of derailment
You see what I meant
The opportunists got on board
Grew fat on the gravy train

Some lionised themselves
Turned the struggle into a possession
Assumed they owned that sacred struggle
Claiming to be the liberators
Others adopted mercenary tendencies

The chasms are widening
The diversionary tactics at play
Hunger and poverty gobbling communities
Opportunists now at each other's throats
Reality check time is now

BAD MOUTH

No one is spared the vitriol
The verbal diarrhoea spewed
Making mountains out of anthills
The dangerous game now played
The many foes now made everywhere
Baying for that ice cold harlot blood
There is the looming gruesome end
The pages of history are littered
With many that fell into disgrace

UNANSWERED QUESTIONS

Taking bootlicking to the higher levels
Sanitising that dark, dank period
Singing all the wrong songs for supper
Rubbishing all that excruciating agony

Taking us for dim wits
With rabbit tail like memories
Abusing those acres of media space
Distorting that very painful story
Many questions yet to be answered

THE MINDLESS OPULENCE

While squalor walks like man
Like a serial killer decimating lives
The State' scarce resources are spent
The profligacy daily displayed
Resources now spent like confetti

Fights over diamond studded rings
The shit spilling into disrespected courts
The brats' alcohol and drug binges
Proving too costly to the weeping nation
The nation still under the steel yoke

The brats turn into braggarts
Taking to social media to display
Displaying the mindless ostentation
Displaying the abundance of arrogance
There in their inherited verbal diarrhoea

WHAT A DISGRACE

And now there is no legacy
Shoved into history's trash can
Jezebel on a war path now
With her scalding words destroying
Availed are the acres of media space
There to belittle all and sundry

Her words are pure venom
That harlot blood boiling
The female version of Rasputin
Tightly gripping those shrivelled balls
Cheered on by power gluttons

O what a big disgrace this is
The poisonous tongue wagging
The shameful opulence displayed
The television philanthropy exhibited
That greed cannot be concealed
Out there in the spotlight it is

THAT STAIN

That dementia displayed
At home and abroad
That bragging long done
Those degrees in violence
That stubborn stain in our minds
With what detergent or stain remover
Will we wash or wish it away

Taking refuge behind the fingers
Gratuitous dispensing of violence
Kindergarten stories of self defence
The myth of invincibility shattered

FALLING

And then you wormed your way
Wormed your way up there
There in the corridors of power
You who left the cosy marital bed
The cosy bed of your marriage
That unbridled lust for power
And the ever available trinkets
Now you shit and piss on us
The fall from grace is near

THE PIRANHAS

Everywhere I turn
Everywhere I look
Everywhere I see them
The piranhas at it

In a feeding frenzy
The unbridled avarice
Chewing each other up
The piranhas at it

Biting off chunks
Ripping each other apart
Rivers of blood flowing
The piranhas at it

CONDEMNED

Once exalted
Now reviled and rejected
Deep down in the dust
Your wretched name
An epitome of soullessness

Your welcome you overstayed
Prayers to the devil you said
That innocent blood you drank
That orgy of senseless killings
Those indelible bitter scars

The castration of the nation
The sacrosanct you profaned
Limbs, lives senselessly lost
Machiavellian schemes manifested
Drown, Narcissus drown

That myth of invincibility shattered
Rot now wicked miscreant rot
Down in the maggot infested dungeon

THEIR ROMP AND POMP

Alligators
The inflamed udder
Of the sacred cow
The defiled village wells
The devil's disciples
Building the nation
With dams of liquor
Gouging gullible minds
The soul shepherds then
Espousing indifference would work
Behind that mindless romp and pomp
The resilience of our African ways

IN THE HEROES ACRE OF THE MIND

THE MESSAGE

Gone against the grain
Shooting the messengers

The message there still
Immortalised by the messengers

Long after the departure
Singers and players of instruments

The message around still
Massaging our eager minds

The dreams, visions, hopes
The compass we still bear

The messages long immortalised
Long before the messengers are interred

For in the beginning was the word
Not the story of the hen and the egg

ANT VOICE

They are too busy
Too busy to listen
They pay dearly
Loud mouthed buffoons
This ant voice warns
No one takes heed
The pay day draws close
The ant voice will be vindicated
Yearning for those luminaries
The likes of Willie Dzawanda Musarurwa
The likes of Geoff Nyarota
The likes of Onesimo Makani Kabweza
The likes of Tich Mukuku
This ant voice speaks still
A captured profession in view
Dabbling in speech journalism
Dabbling in spreading nauseating libel
Employed to trash perceived foes
Just to get the fallen crumbs
From the devil's high tables
And this ant voice warns
Against the prostituting of the profession
The day of reckoning will come
The certainty of the rising sun
Acres of space for vitriolic attacks
While real issues take a back seat
The ant voice will still speak

Pricking the remaining consciences

TIMELESS

And the lyrics maintain the barbed ring
And the message is still ageless
Never to be rendered insipid at all
Such is the power of great works of art
Transcending the artificial segmentation of time
For we are there in the past, present and future

'And when you think its peace and safety a sudden destruction'
And the words retain the barbed ring still
The rampant burning and looting erupting
The heretics will display the medals tomorrow
Perhaps to be cheated again by opportunists
History has this uncanny ability to repeat itself
And my ant voice will be there forever
And the words will retain the barbed ring still

POET IN EXILE

[lines for chenjerai hove]

His voice deemed discordant
Singing all the wrong songs
Not singing the usual platitudes
Taking them out of their comfort zone

In a huff he packed his bags
Baying for his blood they were
The hounds had picked the scent
That audacious eye was too much
That discordant voice had to be silenced

TO DENIS BRUTUS

In the beginning was the word
In the end will be the word
For words you used to confront
Confronting the truncheons
Confronting the racist jack boots
For yours was righteous indignation

Posterity will treasure the words
That struggle is not yet over
'Greed pollutes our planet'
There are the old and new foes
Your words remain our compass

Did you leave poetic attacks on xenophobia
The reversal of the gains of that struggle
You surely must have shed a tear or two
Somewhere on the pages must be the tear drops
The activist in you did not die at all
For the activist in word and deed secured immortality

LINES FOR CHENJERAI HOVE

Now you are at home
At home in exile
That is the conundrum
Then you left
This unbearable psychiatric ward
Hear the demented voices
There in the red hills of home
Those deranging reverberations
The rattling of the bones
'Mapfupa angu achamuka'
Hear the words of that prophetess
That spirit of resilience
Now you are up in arms
Those daggers are drawn
Exile keep your bags packed
Turn ploughshares into swords
This is what time dictates now
And now the poets speak
What is this hen pecking its eggs
I shall remember that incisiveness
Forgetting is a heinous crime

IN THIS BLOOD

In this blood
The thud of the adze
Chipping off the rough edges
That craftsman's inner spirit
Sweetly embedded in that medium
Then mutilated
Then annihilate
'Thou shall not have any other gods'

In this blood
Those songs
The evocation of the spirits
The immense musical appreciation
These are the roots
Posterity shall have not parched throat

TO P. K.

Your part you played
A standing ovation this is
Those sacrifices in Zambia
You could have chosen comfort
Relative middle class comfort

On the side of the downtrodden
You, Joshua Nkomo and many others
The dangers of enemy fire ever present
That racist regime had to be dislodged

You will never walk alone
Ndabaningi Sithole is there with you
Many they have passionately hated
You dared to sing the dirges
Forsaking the fruits of bootlicking
Posterity will treasure those living lessons

TUMULTUOUS TIMES

Then you left in a huff
The living was getting rough
The vortex of violence
The raging fiery inferno
Some say you ran away
The fire razing your home
That you had to extinguish
In the still of the night
You left for another country
That country called exile
There to face horrors of rejection
Family ties brutally severed
The turbulence within
Today tumultuous times still
The news from what was home
What still is home to you
The mind gripped by anxiety
The bags you pack and unpack
Hearing of the fragile peace
Hearing of self-seeking politicians
Your mind in turbulence still
Conflicting stories reverberating
Throwing your mind into a whirlpool
Trying to bridge that gap
The gap between truth and lies
The tumultuous times dog you still
Well you are not alone in this

The tired masses back home wait
Dying in anticipation of respite
Retaining that resilience still
Swallowing that drug called hope
Trying to look back into the future
Yearning for a lustrous future
Wondering whether the trust is misplaced
Wondering whether the leopard changed spots
For the first cut is the deepest
For the cock will always crow
And the dove will always coo
Waiting in anticipation of the good times
When the wounds will heal
When African laughter will resonate
And the world will join in the fun

YET ANOTHER GAP

While you lived
You were a foe
To be persecuted at every turn
Reviled and rejected
For lighting that fire
The fire they claim to have lit
Elbowed you away from the fireside
You then were demonised
For they feared the truth
For your blood they bayed
Their opportunism you exposed
In your death you haunt them
Hurting their inflated egos

That which they now claim to rectify
You had long seen and tried to correct
Their efforts not heartfelt at all
Just another trump card in their game
Enjoying the sound of their voices
They chose not to listen
Haunt them in their commissions
Their hypocrisy cannot be concealed

Like trees that bear no fruit
They shall be cut and burnt
Fools standing lip deep in water
See their parched throats

The warping of your story
That we shall not allow
They shall be found wanting
When their souls are weighed
Shameless masters of double speak
Look at their monuments
The weeds shall choke them
They are like a house built on the sand
You the stone the builder refused
The head corner stone you shall be
The full story not yet told
The nation shall drink
The cool water of the well you dug
Together with others they choose to trash
The fullness of your life is in your death
That is the way of the resilient

THANKING THE LIBERATORS

And then the ululation
The shrill of whistling
The cracking hand clapping
Accompanying the hunters' return

The leaping tongues of fire
The bon fires lit
Stories of triumph told
Spiced by the occasional innocuous lies

The warmth of togetherness
The showers of totemic praises
Stroking the hunters' egos
Then the clangourous din dies

POEMS FROM THE SETTING SUN

AFRICA DAY REFLECTIONS

The bandits came from lands far away
Came from across seas and oceans
Came armed with the maxim gun
Came armed with a warped interpretation
A warped interpretation of the bible
Came to redeem the pagan from himself
The uncivilised with their brand of civilisation
All they did was to satisfy their lust
Raped her and she still bears the scars
The mental and physical scars still there
The raw wounds there to this day

She still is a victim of rape today
Raped repeatedly now by kith and kin
Raped by mercenaries masquerading as liberators
Her children wail with no end in sight
Her children washed away by rivers of squalor
Her children yearning for the sun to shine again
Her children locked in combat with bandits
Those from home and from lands far away

STATE OF THE CONTINENT

A dry barren wind of graft
Blowing across this continent

Nations in turbulence
Flouted constitutions galore

Wave upon wave of conflict
Child soldiers out of this evil womb

Gluttonous megalomaniacs holding on
Losers that will not bow out gracefully

Nations held in captivity
By ghosts of the past

Arms bills sky rocketing
Food allocations nose diving

Nations continually wilting
In the stranglehold of ideas drought

Hailstorms of self-aggrandisement
Continually pummel emasculated populations

Power hungry monsters
Ensconced in the corridors of power

The plundering of nations' wealth
Stashing in foreign bank accounts

Wave upon wave of protests
Dissenting voices brutally crushed

Refugees criss-crossing the continent
Everywhere treated like vermin

The bright rays of undying hope
The slumbering giant now rising

A BRAND NEW DAY

There is this looming vibrancy
A new day is dawning
Birds' songs in the rising sun
And my soul is caressed

Feel the hustle and bustle
For the challenges to be surmounted
Seeking self- liberation as usual
Never again to be a slave
Buried under mounds of repression

Severing those shackles and chains
That is the divine mission
That was never a soap bubble
That was never rainbow in the sky
Hear the ululation for the new day is here

THE WRITING ON THE WALL

By the road side citizens watch
Watching the tragicomedy unfold
Watching a display of ostentation
The flagrant abuse of scarce resources
A shameless display of profligacy

Impecunious and impoverished they watch
Selling their shrivelled vegetables
The consumer class gobbling resources
Not a thought spared for the citizens
The naked profligacy on display

But that deafening silence is gone
No longer are the voices muffled
The hare brained schemes now trashed
The looming implosion and explosion
That emasculation totally rejected

DROPS OF FREEDOM

I hear my dad still saying
'Woza malamulela'
Then I was blind as a bat
Now that veil is off my mind's eye

'Woza malamulela' now I also say
As the pregnant skies open up
Those drops severing this bondage
Severing those devilish schemes

'Woza malamulela' children shout it out
That our people may not be manipulated
Trading their precious votes for food
Voting with their stomachs not minds

'Woza malamulela' we shout it loud and clear
That our people may not be set up against each other
By crooks masquerading as their benefactors
That our people may not be proxy warriors

---

[11] Come relief giver. Translation of the IsiNdebele words in the poem

SEARCHING FOR THE IDEAL

Flood gates closed
Burst the dam wall
Flow to the sea

Caged bird
Fly to the sky
Stretch your wings

Potted plant
Your roots spread
Shatter the vase base

ARISE, AFRIKA ARISE

Siphoning our raw materials still
While in abject poverty we wallow
Taking away our gold, diamonds, platinum
While we adorn our bodies with fake jewellery

Propagating their anglophone ideas
Spreading their francophone thinking
Somewhere lusophone ideas held supreme
African philosophies on the dung heap

The poisoned and stunted present crop
Choosing to forget Marcus Mosiah Garvey
Choosing to forget Kwame Nkrumah
Choosing to remove reggae from the airwaves

That dream should now bear fruit
These chasms have to be bridged
The senseless bickering should now end
Africa with mud and spittle get your sight

WHEN TIME IS UP

Let the maggots feed
Feasting time for them

All comes to nothing
Carefully read Ecclesiastes

Chase away the priest
Drive away the politician

Forsake their speechifying
Abusing the maggots' food

Dance to those songs
Eat to your heart's content

WORKERS' DAY THOUGHTS

Drenched to the marrow
The acid rain of abject poverty
The napalm bombs of hunger
Vibrations of despondency everywhere
The quick sand of mass unemployment
The deafening silence of factory sirens
The debilitating emasculation gripping
In the stranglehold of uncertainties
The shrinking and uncertain pay packets
In illicit brews drowning sorrows
Trapped in the hyacinth of escapism

CLEAR SKIES

There is this whirlwind
Dust in our eyes
Many stumble while others fall

There is this hailstorm
The leaves torn to shreds
Next is harvest of thorns

These empty granaries see
The skies with-hold the rains
A debilitating drought set in

See the raging storm
The drifting grey clouds
Giving way to clear skies

THE SUN LONG SET

The sale by date is gone
The sun long set
The dementia has set in
Someone did not tell the emperor
Tell the emperor of his nudity
Is it the warmth in that cocoon
Shielding you from the nauseating poverty
Not seeing those yawning shells
That were once thriving factories
The ever escalating mass unemployment
That to you is evidence of progress
When home is now not habitable
That your brats live next door
You do not see the conspicuous hypocrisy
Blind to your double standards
The dementia long took root
Heidi Holland was spot on after all

THAT DAY IS COMING

Yesterday you were at it
Chasing villagers out of their homes
With your newly found power
You chased after the diamonds
With not a trace of decency
Placed on Mount Kilimanjaro the greed
Placed in the spotlight the degree in violence
That lust for power taking centre stage
Forgot that every dog has its day
And that day is not very far

THAT DAY IS COMING [PART TWO]

Afflicted by delusions
Under the blanket of illusions
In a deep slumber
Under estimating the people
See this inferno rising
The people are speaking
The people will always speak
They have always spoken

Where are the listeners
That meekness mistaken for weakness
The seething intangible indignation
A non-existent hidden hand blamed
The time of reckoning is nigh
That pool of patience is running dry
Now breaking the walls of fear
Look, look that day is at hand

AFTER THE STORM

About the golden sunsets
And the cry of the fish eagle
In the mystical, mythical Lake Kariva[2]
That I shall write about

About the mighty Zambezi
And the awe inspiring Falls
And that smoke that thunders
That is shall sing about

About the searing heat
And those hot springs-Tshipise
There in the Vhembe valley
That I shall talk about

About the undulating landscape
There in the Eastern Highlands
Those perennial life filled showers
And the lush green vegetation

Like one with a parched throat
After a long and winding walk
Across the desert of repression
To my heart's content I drink

---

[2]Kariba

CLEANING THE TOILET

The putrid, acrid smell
Those hairy maggots
There on the stale shit
In the rivers of urine
Defunct flushing unit
In dire need of cleaning
Then I must clean the toilet

Typhoid, dysentery, cholera
Decimating the future
Get the flushing unit working
This toilet we must clean
The moment demands decision
Not the time to duck and dive

THE SPIRITUAL DIMENSION

DAGGERS DRAWN

God is out if it
Watching the isms and schisms
There in the spotlight
Taking centre stage

Protestant god at it
Catholic god at it
Papal infallibility questioned
New paths charted

Lessons of love abandoned
Gods of petrol bombs worshipped
Gods of missiles worshipped
That is the essence

Fighting to please peace loving gods
Killing in the name of god
Did god make man in his own image
Its man making god in his image
The emptiness of it plain to see
The bottomless pit of doctrines

BACK HANDER

Not throwing the baby out
Out with the bath water
'Speak tongue's lash
On the naked buttocks of silence'
Reality delivering a back hander
On the jaws of half truths

Flocking in multitudes to those places
There to be fed on sexist doctrines
Men clinging to the pulpit
Reviling women for the menstrual cycle
Preaching messages of subjugation

Branding sex as sin
Hiding under false cloaks of celibacy
Many an altar boy sodomised
Many a married woman enticed
Enticed into breaking those vows

There beneath the podiums
Used as cannon fodder
Dictated to by the minority
Chasms born out of petty jealousies
While male dominance grows
The podium and the pulpit
Weapons in the hands of a few

VEILED EYES

Having gobbled the diet
The befuddling diet of religions
Having swallowed hook, line and sinker
The gospel of stunting apostasy
Now with their warped minds
They denigrate themselves unwittingly
Enveloped by the darkness of foolishness

The essence of our ways is warped
Labelling our ways ancestral worship
Conveniently forgetting our intercessors
Hacking at the roots of our confidence
Defiling all our sacrosanct shrines
But the resilience is plain to see

INDIFFERENCE

Beggar's artful voice modulations
Pricks not long lost conscience
The hardness of cold steel
That is the scheme of things
The beggar chants the refrain
'*Upenyu hwakasiyana siyana*'[3]
Chill gusts of indifference blow
Maybe some consciences are pricked
Still the beggar flaunts his artistry
The beggar's observation in his finger tips
There is that deep chasm
The distance between his needs and my wants
Am I not my brother's keeper
Songs of sorrow issue from the pavements
Behind these lines the pity and disgust

---

[3] Life is different for different individuals

DAVID DEADSTONE[4]

In an ominous silence
There before your discovery
Your out of place imposing statue
There before that rumbling
The rumbling mosi-oa-tunya

The BaTonga did not matter
That name refused to die
Under the English dead weight of queen Victoria
Your queen could not take precedence

Mine was righteous indignation
Stood there and told you the truth
Your imposing statue at that place
That out of place statue

---

[4] David Livingstone

SHIP IN A STORM

This ship battered
Battered by the angry sea
The raging storm
Calm shall return
Safely on shore

This ship tossed
Threatened by angry waves
At the risk of disintegrating
Calm shall return
It was long decreed

This ship is captained
Captained by the greatest
He who commands the winds
Whose voice is heard by waves
Whose voice calms storms

There shall be calm
After the raging storm
The waves heed the command
Of He who is omnipotent
He who is the beginning and the end

DESPERADOS[5]

Under a torrent of blows
Avalanche of desperation
And the evident gullibility
Miracle solutions offered
And the sheep are lost
Lost in the thick mist of confusion

Plunged further into poverty
Con artists everywhere sprouting
Like mushrooms after the rains
Hoping for miraculous solutions
Under the hypnosis of gods

---

[5] Criminals/ outlaws

DEFILED TEMPLE

They have defiled the temple
We now have to cleanse the temple
We must now wield the whip
Drive out the muck from the Lord's house

In the name of the Lord they trade
Selling all kinds of wares
We must now uproot the corruption
Drive out the stench of corruption

They shall be put to shame
All who steal in his name
All who rob and oppress the poor
They shall be put to shame

They are in stinking opulence
Leading the Lord's flock astray
Where will the wolves run to
All those clad in sheep skins

MEIN KAMPF[6]

That is the fight
Against their doctrines
Against isms and schisms
Refusing to be shackled
Refusing to be chained

Politicians and priests at it
Wielding fear against them
Fear of the unknown
That is what we fight against

Battle for my spirituality
Battle against domination
Dominated by pulpit and podium
That is my biggest fight
This will forever be my fight

---

[6]My struggle. Title of book written by Adolf Hitler

TO GODS

In each breath are the gods
Mostly the craven ones
False deities seeking power
I have seen the money gods
Social, political gods abound

Everywhere you turn there are gods
Gods that reap, reap, reap
Gods that reap without ever sowing
The ubiquitous and deranged gods
Everywhere gods afflicted by dementia

I have seen gods like mushrooms
Everywhere the gods are sprouting
Facebook, twitter, whatsapp gods
The gods holding our minds captive
Gods immersed in unbridled avarice

ANOTHER STORM

Engulfed we are
Violent storms of deception
Ensnared we are
Succulent traps of advertisement

Lost in the thick mist of materialism
Pummelled by hailstorms
Hail storms of self -denigration
The negation of spiritualism

This is the age of scientific proof
This is the age of one dimension
Reduced to automatons we have been
A speck of reality this is

In floods of mindless ostentation
That is where we are firmly rooted
We the architects of our demise
Liberate ourselves from this dungeon we must
Shape our destiny we must
In this forge of repression

OFF YOUR HIGH HORSE

Get off your high horse
Spit your caustic arrogance
Eat now humble pie
Time demands that of you
That reggae great showed the way
'He who hide the wrong he did
Surely did the wrong thing still'

Mend those broken fences
Repair those bombed bridges
Drop now that heavy baggage
Free yourself from the prison
That prison of false pride
Just one word is the master key

The ghosts of the past haunt you
Sever those shackles and chains
Those that keep you from eternal bliss
That keep your soul in the dungeon
The dungeon of your vanity
You, thirsty while deep in water

MIXED BAG

BULL ON THE RAMPAGE
[Solidarity with Mzansi folk]

That mad bull on the rampage
Gored those young lives
Leaving mothers submerged in tears
Fathers on the tenterhooks

Driven by an immense sense of justice
They challenged the racist system
Dared to challenge that hegemony
Took that dehumanisation head on

Those young lives were mowed
Many died in that lead hailstorm
Kill them before they grow
Nip that revolution in the bud

That blood was not shed in vain
Not even CODESA can hold it back
That mighty force lives on still
Not one warped family can stall it

OUT OF THE CLOSET

Today the sycophantic press sings
Singing all the wrong songs
Singing for their supper and free beer
The peanuts you throw about like confetti
For all the willing pet monkeys

Today they fall over each other
Just to get the falling crumbs
Augmenting their paltry pay packets
Trampling their own consciences
Abusing the power society bestows

Tomorrow they will know
The sex for jobs scandals
The sex for stage appearance debauchery
When the closet gets too full
The avalanche of falling skeletons

ICC
[International Criminal Conspiracy]

Setting the record straight
Aware of the heinous crimes
The many acts of genocide
The many criminals in hiding
There in the corridors of power
Not an apologist for them
The facts are plain to see

Blair is out there having fun
George Bush too in lots of bliss
Those blatant lies were the pretext
Saddam Hussein lies in his grave
Fell to Anglo-Saxon diabolic conspiracies
But the war criminals go scot-free

The international criminal conspiracy
An extension of those unholy alliances
The kingpins remain unaccounted for
The proxies are taken to the Hague
The words of that great African ring true
'Justice is greater than the law'

UNTITLED

Deserted by sleep
Eyes on TV screen glued
Spewing nauseating propaganda
The grand schemes supported
Here the truth is warped
To suit military – industrial schemes

The Palestinians still pummelled
Still rendered homeless
Perhaps the Libyans now regret
The loss of the benevolent dictator
While the Iraqis wake up
From the blatant obscene lies
For there were no weapons of mass destruction

The looting continues unabated
There in the mineral rich jungles
See the beneficiaries of fratricide
The DRC still knows no peace

Still deserted by sleep
Wondering where the truth lies
About radical economic transformation
While crime rises in the slums
With xenophobia showing the blindness
Economic apartheid ever escalating

Watching the bickering back home
All the talk about regime change
The tragicomedy now unfolding
As the sun is now setting
Hear the eerie hooting of owls
The ominous laughing of hyenas
And vultures waiting for the carrion
Weep no more land of my birth

Refusing now to be in shackles
The shackles of self-denigration
Packaged as the gospel truth

Publisher's list

If you have enjoyed *Righteous Indignation* consider these other fine books from Mwanaka Media and Publishing:

Cultural Hybridity and Fixity by Andrew Nyongesa
The Water Cycle by Andrew Nyongesa
Tintinnabulation of Literary Theory by Andrew Nyongesa
I Threw a Star in a Wine Glass by Fethi Sassi
South Africa and United Nations Peacekeeping Offensive Operations by Antonio Garcia
Africanization and Americanization Anthology Volume 1, Searching for Interracial, Interstitial, Intersectional and Interstates Meeting Spaces, Africa Vs North America by Tendai R Mwanaka
A Conversation…, A Contact by Tendai Rinos Mwanaka
A Dark Energy by Tendai Rinos Mwanaka
Africa, UK and Ireland: Writing Politics and Knowledge Production Vol 1 by Tendai R Mwanaka
Best New African Poets 2017 Anthology by Tendai R Mwanaka and Daniel Da Purificacao
Keys in the River: New and Collected Stories by Tendai Rinos Mwanaka
Logbook Written by a Drifter by Tendai Rinos Mwanaka
Mad Bob Republic: Bloodlines, Bile and a Crying Child by TendaiRinos Mwanaka
*How The Twins Grew Up/Makurire Akaita Mapatya*by Milutin Djurickovic and Tendai Rinos Mwanaka
Writing Language, Culture and Development, Africa Vs Asia Vol 1 by Tendai R Mwanaka, Wanjohi wa Makokha and Upal Deb
Zimbolicious Poetry Vol 1 by Tendai R Mwanaka and Edward Dzonze

Zimbolicious: An Anthology of Zimbabwean Literature and Arts, Vol 3 by Tendai Mwanaka

Under The Steel Yoke by Jabulani Mzinyathi

A Case of Love and Hate by Chenjerai Mhondera

Epochs of Morning Light by Elena Botts

Fly in a Beehive by Thato Tshukudu

Bounding for Light by Richard Mbuthia

White Man Walking by John Eppel

A Cat and Mouse Affair by Bruno Shora

Sentiments by Jackson Matimba

Best New African Poets 2018 Anthology by Tendai R Mwanaka and Nsah Mala

Drawing Without Licence by Tendai R Mwanaka

Writing Grandmothers/Escribiendo sobrenu estras raíces: Africa Vs Latin America Vol 2 by Tendai R Mwanaka and Felix Rodriguez

The Scholarship Girl by Abigail George

Words That Matter by Gerry Sikazwe

The Gods Sleep Through It by Wonder Guchu

The Ungendered by Delia Watterson

The Big Noise and Other Noises by Christopher Kudyahakudadirwe

Tiny Human Protection Agency by Megan Landman

Ghetto Symphony by Mandla Mavolwane

Sky for a Foreign Bird by Fethi Sassi

A Portrait of Defiance by Tendai Rinos Mwanaka

When Escape Becomes the only Lover by Tendai R Mwanaka

Where I Belong: moments, mist and song by Smeetha Bhoumik

Soon to be released
Of Bloom Smoke by Abigail George

Denga reshiri yokunze kwenyika by Fethi Sassi

Nationalism: (Mis)Understanding   Donald Trump's Capitalism, Racism, Global Politics, International Trade and Media Wars, Africa Vs North America Vol 2 by Tendai R Mwanaka

Ashes by Ken Weene and Umar O. Abdul

Ouafa and Thawra: About a Lover From Tunisia by Arturo Desimone

Thoughts Hunt The Loves/Pfungwa Dzinovhima Vadiwa by Jeton Kelmendi

واويَسهَرُ اللَّيلُ عَلى شَفَتي...وَالغَمامُby Fethi Sassi

A Letter to the President by Mbizo Chirasha

Litany of a Foreign Wife by Nnane Ntube

Notes From a Modern Chimurenga: Collected Stories by Tendai Rinos Mwanaka

Tom Boy by Megan Landman

My Spiritual Journey: A Study of the Emerald Tablets by Jonathan Thompson

https://facebook.com/MwanakaMediaAndPublishing/

Printed in the United States
By Bookmasters